A BULLY–FREE BUS

Text by Pamela Hall
Illustrations by Bob Ostrom

Content Consultant
Finessa Ferrell, Director,
National Center for School Engagement

visit us at www.abdopublishing.com

Published by Magic Wagon, a division of the ABDO Group, PO Box 398166, Minneapolis, MN 55439. Copyright © 2013 by Abdo Consulting Group, Inc. International copyrights reserved in all countries. All rights reserved. No part of this book may be reproduced in any form without written permission from the publisher.

Looking Glass Library™ is a trademark and logo of Magic Wagon.

Printed in the United States of America, North Mankato, Minnesota.
032012
092012

 THIS BOOK CONTAINS AT LEAST 10% RECYCLED MATERIALS.

Text by Pamela Hall
Illustrations by Bob Ostrom
Edited by Holly Saari
Design and production by Craig Hinton

Library of Congress Cataloging-in-Publication Data

Hall, Pamela, 1961-
  A bully-free bus / by Pamela Hall ; illustrated by Bob Ostrom ; content consultant, Finessa Ferrell.
    p. cm. -- (A bully-free world)
  ISBN 978-1-61641-844-1
  1. Bullying--Prevention--Juvenile literature. 2. Bullying in schools--Juvenile literature. 3. School buses--Safety measures--Juvenile literature. 4. Travel etiquette--Juvenile literature. 5. Aggressiveness in children--Juvenile literature. I. Ostrom, Bob. II. Title.
  BF637.B85H335 2013
  371.5'8--dc23
                                                        2011038551

JNF
371.58
HALL

TABLE OF CONTENTS

BULLYING
ON THE BUS

Bullies choose to be mean. Why do they do that? Bullies are angry. They let their anger out by hurting others. Why does bullying happen on the bus? All ages of kids are on the bus. It is easy for older kids to pick on younger kids. And, the bus is a small place. There is nowhere to hide on a moving bus.

The bus is the third most popular place for kids to bully. The kids on Bus 21 are bullying each other. Come along as they clean up their bad behavior and make their bus bully-free!

HITTING AND SHOVING

Kids might push or hit others on the bus. This is called physical bullying. That is when someone touches another person in a harmful way. Sarah sits behind Ava. She smacks Ava on the head a lot. Ava's head hurts. Ava is scared, too. What can she do?

WHAT TO DO

Sarah has no right to hit Ava. What should Ava do? First, she should not hit back. Fighting back makes bullying worse. She could get hurt. Hitting Sarah would make Ava a bully, too. Ava doesn't want that.

Second, Ava needs to tell an adult she trusts. It must be someone she feels comfortable with. It could be her bus driver or a cafeteria worker. This isn't tattling. This is called reporting. The adult will help stop Sarah from bullying.

SEAT HOG

Bullies act mean to get attention. Lots of bullies don't get the attention they need at home. Joe is mean on the bus so he gets noticed. He hogs the back seats. He doesn't let anyone else in the back row. Derek is sick of it. What can he do?

WHAT TO DO

First, Derek should ask his friends to join him. There is power in numbers. Then he should tell Joe he is being rude. Derek and his friends don't have to take it anymore. When Joe sees them, he knows he is beat. Derek and his friends have the power now, not Joe.

TAKING YOUR STUFF

Bullies think they can take stuff that belongs to other people. But, they have no right to touch others or their things. That is a form of physical bullying, too. It hurts as much as getting punched or kicked.

Tim doesn't like the bus. He is often a victim of bullying. Carlos takes Tim's stuff a lot. What can Tim do?

WHAT TO DO

First, Tim needs to stand up for himself. Tim should look Carlos in the eye. He can say, "Stop! You can't touch my things."

Then Tim should ignore Carlos and talk to his friends. Six out of ten elementary students have bullied others. Tim doesn't want to be a bully back to Carlos. Instead, Tim should report Carlos when he gets to school. Carlos will learn that he will get in trouble for bullying.

NAME-CALLING

No one likes to be called names. Name-calling and teasing are ways of verbal bullying. Mean words can hurt as much as getting punched. Bullies say things they know will hurt other people. This makes them feel better about themselves.

Lee calls Isabel names every day. Emily knows this hurts Isabel's feelings. What can Emily do to help Isabel?

WHAT TO DO

Being an upstander is one important way to stop bullying. It is up to Emily to help Isabel. Emily should tell Lee to stop saying mean things. Emily needs to look her right in the eye. She should be firm. She could say, "You can't talk to Isabel like that."

By being an upstander, Emily stands up to Lee. This shows Lee she can't scare them. Lee will quit bullying when she sees no one is bothered by it anymore.

TAKE THE
BULLY TEST

How can you tell if you ever bully? You are a bully if you do things you know will hurt people or make them feel bad. Ask yourself these questions:

Do I feel better when I hurt other kids or take their stuff?

Do I use my strength or size to get my way?

Do I like to leave others out to make them feel bad?

Have I ever spread a rumor that I knew was not true?

Do I like teasing others?

Is it funny to me when I see other kids getting made fun of?

Have I ever kicked, punched, or hit someone?

If you answered "yes" to any of these questions, you might be a bully. Is that really how you want to be?

Of course not! Everyone makes mistakes. You can change the way you act. The first step is to say, "I'm sorry." Practice being nice to other people. Think before you say or do something. Treat others the way you want to be treated.

NOTE TO PARENTS AND CAREGIVERS

Young children often imitate their parents' or caregivers' behaviors. If you show bullying actions or use bullying language, it is likely your children will, too. They do not know their behavior is unacceptable because they see it in trusted adults. You can help prevent your student from bullying by modeling good behavior.

WORDS TO KNOW

physical bullying—pushing, kicking, hitting, or touching someone in a harmful way.

reporting—telling an adult about being bullied.

upstander—someone who sees bullying and stands up for the person being bullied.

verbal bullying—being mean to someone using words, such as by name-calling.

victim—a person who is hurt or suffers due to the actions of another person or outside force.

WEB SITES

To learn more about bullying on the bus, visit ABDO Group online at **www.abdopublishing.com**. Web sites about bullying on the bus are featured on our Book Links page. These links are routinely monitored and updated to provide the most current information available.